better together*

*** This book is best read together, grownup and kid.**

a
kids
book
about

a kids book about

MASCULINITY

by Next Gen Men

A Kids Co.
Editor Emma Wolf
Designer Jelani Memory
Creative Director Rick DeLucco
Studio Manager Kenya Feldes
Sales Director Melanie Wilkins
Head of Books Jennifer Goldstein
CEO and Founder Jelani Memory

DK
Delhi Technical Team Bimlesh Tiwary Pushpak Tyagi, Rakesh Kumar
Senior Production Editor Jennifer Murray
Senior Production Controller Louise Minihane
Senior Acquisitions Editor Katy Flint
Acquisitions Project Editor Sara Forster
Managing Art Editor Vicky Short
Managing Director, Licensing Mark Searle

First American edition, 2025
Published in the United States by DK Publishing, 1745 Broadway, 20th Floor,
New York, NY 10019

First published in Great Britain in 2025 by
Dorling Kindersley Limited, 20 Vauxhall Bridge Road, London SW1V 2SA
A Penguin Random House Company

The authorised representative in the EEA is
Dorling Kindersley Verlag GmbH. Arnulfstr. 124, 80636 Munich, Germany

A catalog record for this book is available from the Library of Congress.
A CIP catalogue record for this book is available from the British Library.
ISBN: 978-0-2417-4389-8

DK books are available at special discounts when purchased in bulk for sales
promotions, premiums, fund-raising, or education use. For details, contact:
DK Publishing Special Markets, 1745 Broadway, 20th Floor, New York, NY 10019
SpecialSales@dk.com

Printed and bound in China
www.dk.com
akidsco.com

MIX
Paper | Supporting
responsible forestry
FSC™ C018179

This book was made with Forest
Stewardship Council™ certified
paper – one small step in DK's
commitment to a sustainable future.
**Learn more at www.dk.com/uk/
information/sustainability**

Dedicated to Shaquille and Bryson.

You shone.

Intro
for grownups

What does it mean to be a good man? How do we raise the next generation to be the curious, compassionate, and courageous young men the world needs today?

These days, a lot of people are talking about what masculinity means, but not enough of us are talking about it with young people themselves. At Next Gen Men, we believe that boys don't need to be taught to be true to themselves, support the people around them, or advocate for gender justice—they just need to be given permission.

This book exists to debunk the rigid cultural narrative about masculinity, and what it has meant to "be a man." We hope to encourage boys and masculine-exploring kids to figure out what masculinity means to them—even when it's hard.

And if you're a grownup reading this, well, that goes for you, too.

Masculinity is a story we tell ourselves, and one that is told to us.

In this book, I'll be telling you a story of masculinity from my perspective.

HI,
my name is Jonathon.

I love rock climbing.

I have a Siberian husky named Delta.

I know how to do a
backflip off of a swing set.*

I'm also very caring and gentle.

My favorite nail polish color is red.

I enjoyed ballet when I was a kid.

*Don't try this without a grownup's permission.

When I was growing up, a lot of people talked to me about masculinity...

and it wasn't always in nice ways.

A lot of the time what I learned about masculinity sounded like...

"GET BIGGER MUSCLES."

"TOUGHEN UP!"

"BOYS DON'T CRY."

"CUT YOUR HAIR, YOU LOOK LIKE A GIRL."

"BOYS DON'T WEAR NAIL POLISH."

The way I learned about masculinity could have been **OPEN** and **AFFIRMING**.

Instead, it was usually
CONTROLLING and **HURTFUL.**

I was told that there was only 1 way to be a boy—and that I was doing it

WRO

ONG.

I know now that we should be writing our own stories.

But it's something I didn't
always know how to do.

And if you feel that way too, that's

OK!

The truth is that what it means to be a man can be a hard thing to figure out.

Many people have their own ideas about what masculinity should be.

I'm curious...what do you think of when you think of masculinity?

What do you think masculinity looks like? What does it sound like?

Turn to the person you're reading with and share what you're thinking about.

And then, ask them about masculinity when they were your age.

What did being a boy look like?

What were the stories they were told?

Are there similarities?

How about differences?

Here's the deal:

WHEN YOU WERE BORN, YOU ENTERED THIS WORLD AS AN AMAZING HUMAN, FULL OF POTENTIAL.

But way before you were born, without you being asked, all of these ideas and expectations existed about the kind of person you should be.

These ideas weren't based on your personal goals, loves, dislikes, or what made you happy.

They were formed based on made-up rules for only boys and girls.

Rules exist for many different reasons.

Some are really good, like how to respect the people around you or how to take care of your family pet.

But some rules exist just to create winners and losers.

This creates a divide between people.

And the catch with masculinity is that when we only follow rigid, unmoving rules about what it means to be a man,

EVERYONE LOSES—

including me and you.

Let me give you an example.

When I was your age, I liked to dance.

I took dance classes and practiced in my room.

I bought specific clothes to wear.

And then...my friends found out.

And they didn't think it
was as cool as I did.

They made fun of me,
and they laughed at me.

I understood loud and clear:

BOYS S
NOT
INTERES
DAN

SHOULD
BE
STED IN
ICE.

Long story short: I gave it up.

I lost a meaningful
form of self-expression.

My peers lost a sense of
trust with each other, that
we could all be celebrated
for our unique interests.

The world lost just a bit
of beauty and magic.

Oh, and one more thing.

When dance is seen as inappropriate for boys because it's something girls do, there's a bigger problem.

Because the meaning isn't just,
"You're a **BOY**, so don't be a girl."

It's also, "Girls are **INFERIOR**."

So even when the rules are about what boys can and can't do, girls and people of other genders lose out too.

I feel like there's a

BETTER

don't you?

WAY...

Not a world with winners and losers, but one where everyone has permission to be themselves.

What if...

THERE WERE NO RULES?!

What if masculinity wasn't 1 single thing that you were either doing "wrong" or doing "right," but rather something unique to you that you choose?

Your masculinity could be different from mine, from your neighbors', from your siblings', or from every person you know.

And that's a great thing.

Because if we get to write our own stories, we

can be a lot more than what we've been told.

Boys can be _____.

CREATIVE
FOCUSED
HUMBLE
CURIOUS
PATIENT

CAPABLE
RESILIENT
FLEXIBLE
STRONG
GENTLE

RESOURCEFUL
DETERMINED
SUPPORTIVE
BRAVE
LOVING
SENSITIVE
FORGIVING

FAIR
LOYAL
HOPEFUL
DEPENDABLE
EMPATHETIC
COMPASSIONATE
GENEROUS

HONEST
TRUSTING
THOUGHTFUL
EXPRESSIVE
CONFIDENT
ENTHUSIASTIC
MAGIC
FUN

INTROSPECTIVE
OPEN-MINDED
TRUSTWORTHY
PRESENT
GROUNDED
ACCEPTING
DECISIVE
GRATEFUL

We get to choose what masculinity means to us.

What does it mean to you?

Outro
for grownups

You know the saying: boys will be boys. But boys will also become men. What if we stayed connected to boys and helped them become their best selves as they grow up?

In everything we do at Next Gen Men, one thing has always been clear: relationship is the medium through which all positive development takes place. This book will only help boys uncover their truest selves if they are held in steady, sensitive, and committed relationships by the people who matter most.

Grownups, that's on you. The young person next to you needs your time, your attention, and your affirmation. After all, boys will be... whatever we give them the space to be.

About The Author

Next Gen Men is a nonprofit organization changing the way we see, act, and think about masculinity. This book, like everything we do, was a collective effort.

Jake Stika (he/him) co-founded Next Gen Men in order to build a future in which boys and men experience less pain, and cause less harm. He's 6'8" and dedicated his younger life to basketball.

Jonathon Reed (he/him) works tirelessly to support the positive development of masculine-identifying youth, and designs resources and trainings for the parents, educators, and coaches who work alongside them.

Veronika Elyk (she/her) is an empathy-driven architect for men's grassroots involvement in the world of gender-based violence prevention and advocacy. She would move mountains for her beloved pitbull, Sarge.

 @nextgenmen   nextgenmen.ca

About The Author

Next Gen Men is a nonprofit organization changing the way we see, act, and think about masculinity. This book, like everything we do, was a collective effort.

Jake Stika (he/him) co-founded Next Gen Men in order to build a future in which boys and men experience less pain, and cause less harm. He's 6'8" and dedicated his younger life to basketball.

Jonathon Reed (he/him) works tirelessly to support the positive development of masculine-identifying youth, and designs resources and trainings for the parents, educators, and coaches who work alongside them.

Veronika Elyk (she/her) is an empathy-driven architect for men's grassroots involvement in the world of gender-based violence prevention and advocacy. She would move mountains for her beloved pitbull, Sarge.

 @nextgenmen   nextgenmen.ca

Made to empower.

    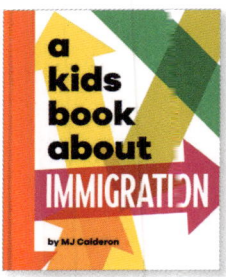

 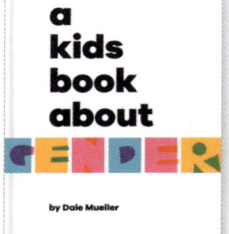 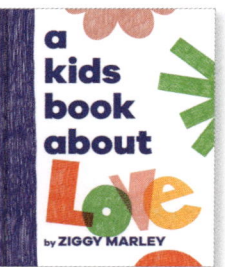 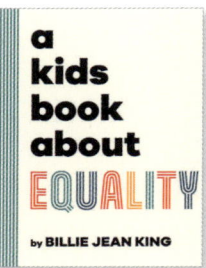 

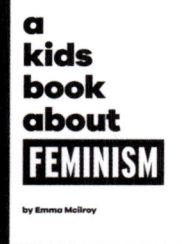 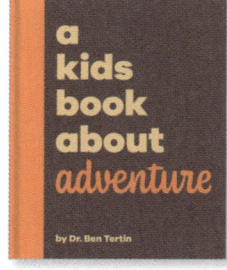 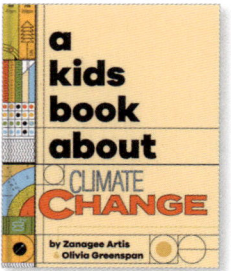